Cursing with Style

A Dicktionary of Expletives

Erika M. Weinert

Cursing with Style: A Dicktionary of Expletives
Published by The Werd Nerd

The content contained herein may not be suitable for all audiences. Reader discretion is advised.

ISBN: 978-0-578-29640-1
Reference/Dictionaries

Cover image (coffeegirl) by [lucky2084] © 123RF.com
Cover design by dbdonovan and Victoria Wolf.
Interior book design by Victoria Wolf, wolfdesignandmarketing.com.

Quantity Purchases: Companies, professional groups, clubs, and other organizations may qualify for special terms when ordering quantities of this title. For information, email thewerdnerdediting@gmail.com.

The
Werd
Nerd

This book is dedicated to my dad,
the late David K. Moberg, who was
as foulmouthed as they come.

INTRODUCTION

When I was a young girl, I wanted to be a renowned author of fiction. Now I edit fiction, and I'm not disappointed.

Editors and established authors know that consistency is a crucial element in the writing and editing process, but newer writers may not. If a manuscript you're writing or editing is sprinkled with *shits*, *damns*, *bitches*, and *fucks*, this book is for you.

As you read through *Cursing with Style*, you'll notice there are variations of the above-mentioned naughty words. It's up to the author to choose one of them and use it consistently. Readers don't want to see *shit show* on page 89 and *shit-show* on page 106. In this book you'll find that it can be written one of three ways—*shitshow* (one word), *shit show* (two words), or *shit-show* (hyphenated)—and again, it's up to the author to choose one spelling of a word and use it consistently throughout their book.

I've been told there are too many variations of *fuck* in this book—*fuckface*, *clusterfuck*, *fuck-ton*, and *mindfuck*, to name a few—but, as an editor who has had to look up each and every one of those damn words while editing manuscripts, I say fuck that!

Cursing with Style began as a spreadsheet which I used as a style guide for expletives while copy and line editing fiction. I kept adding to it while reading through multiple sources dedicated to sweary language until I decided enough was enough. The sources I was combing through were either severely lacking, not specific to US English, or both, so my spreadsheet eventually became *Cursing with Style*—a book I can solely reference going forward. I hope fellow editors will feel the same way about this dicktionary of expletives. It's a go-to guide for all things sweary and vulgar, so you're fucking welcome!

This is not an all-inclusive list, so if you don't find a word you're looking for, oh fucking well!

(MOSTLY)
ALL
THE
SWEAR
WORDS

A

abso-fucking-lutely

Part of Speech: adverb

Definition: a variant of the word *absolutely*, which is an affirmative reply to a question but with more enthusiasm—more gusto!

Remarks: I *abso-fucking-lutely* love this word, so I'm glad it's the first on the list of many expletives.

Without the hyphens, it takes a minute for readers to know what they're looking at. You want your audience to be able to read your work without getting tripped up, and hyphenation provides a seamless read.

A

apeshit

Part of Speech: adjective

Definition: describes when a person rages out like an angry monkey throwing its feces.

Remarks: My mom is gonna go *apeshit* when she finds out I wrote a book of expletives.

A

ass/-ass

Part of Speech: noun/suffix

Definition: *n.* a person's backside, butt/buttocks; an imbecile; also a donkey, but who in the hell calls a donkey an *ass* these days?

suffix. -*ass* can be added to the ends of words as an intensifier, such as *smart-ass*, *cold-ass*, *big-ass*, *sweet-ass*, and *crazy-ass*.

Remarks: The possibilities are endless with *ass* as a suffix—or a prefix, such as *asswipe* or *asshole*!

A

assclown

Part of Speech: noun

Definition: someone who has no idea what the fuck they're talking about, and everyone knows it but them.

Remarks: This word went viral after audiences went apeshit over the 1999 movie *Office Space*, in which one of the main characters calls a famous singer a "no-talent *assclown*."

A

assface

Part of Speech: noun

Definition: a person who is loathsome.

Remarks: You may be tempted to format this as two words, but as one word, it provides clarity for your audience.

A

assfuck

Part of Speech: verb

Definition: to perform anal sex, but I've also heard it as an exclamation.

Remarks: I contemplated not including this word in the book, but it's an expletive, and I want to be as all-inclusive as possible.

A

assgoblin/ass goblin

Part of Speech: noun

Definition: someone who munches butt or engages in anal sex; just a general put-down of a person, like *asshole.*

Remarks: I haven't heard anyone use this word in quite some time. It can be written as one word or two, but you can't have it both ways. Maintain consistency by choosing only one way of spelling it.

A

asshat

Part of Speech: noun

Definition: an annoying and/or stupid person, pretty much the same as *asshole*.

Remarks: Don't be an *asshat*! Read this book all the way through . . . because the word *asshole* is next.

A

asshole

Part of Speech: noun

Definition: other than the part of the body where our waste is excreted, this can be a person—a detestable person—who lacks decency, class, and sense.

Remarks: You're an *asshole* if you don't read all of the entries in this book.

A

asswipe

Part of Speech: noun

Definition: a person–a detestable person–who lacks decency, class, and sense.

Remarks: This may have the same definition as the word *asshole*, but in my opinion, calling a person an *asswipe* is more powerful than calling them an *asshole*. It just leaves a stronger sting afterward.

B

badass

Part of Speech: noun/adjective

Definition: *n.* a troublemaker; someone who has exceptional skill.

adj. ready to make some trouble and get rowdy; having an awesome skill set; describes a noun and typically comes before or after the noun it describes, such as *badass* editor, but can also be used on its own.

Remarks: You're such a *badass* for buying this book!

badassery

Part of Speech: noun

Definition: simply stated, it's being a badass; a frightfully impressive badass quality.

Remarks: I don't get off on flaunting my *badassery*; I'm a humble woman.

B

bastard

Part of Speech: noun

Definition: the child of an unmarried couple; a rude insult that has nothing to do with the first definition–kind of like saying *asshole* or similar.

Remarks: Calling someone a *bastard* because their parents weren't married when they were born isn't really common anymore, and it's fucking rude, so don't do it.

B

batshit

Part of Speech: adjective/adverb

Definition: *adj*. absolutely fucking bonkers, irrational, and/or senseless.

adv. describing an adjective, like the ones listed in the definition above (e.g., *batshit* crazy).

Remarks: I've heard my colleagues say they have *batshit* clients. So far, I've been lucky in that respect.

big-ass

Part of Speech: adjective

Definition: bigger than big, massive; emphasizing just how ginormous something is, and typically followed by a noun.

Remarks: Someday I'd like a house with a *big-ass* pool in the backyard.

B

bitch (biatch)

Part of Speech: noun/verb

Definition: *n.* an insult directed toward someone to insinuate they are mean, spiteful, or offensive in some way; something that's difficult or arduous in some way; can also be a complaint.

v. moaning and groaning, complaining about something.

Remarks: This word can be manipulated in multiple ways, such as by adding a *y* at the end to get the adjective *bitchy*, or by adding *ass* and *boy* at the end to get the nouns *bitchass* and *bitchboy*. There's also the present participle verb *bitching*, which I sometimes tend to do when I don't get my way. Yeah, I can be a little *biatch* sometimes. Let's not forget the word *bitchface*, which is coming up soon.

B

bitchass/bitch-ass

Part of Speech: noun/adjective

Definition: *n.* a coward who appears tough at first until someone gets real with them; then they become a wimp.

adj. compound adjective that describes a person as cowardly; punk-ass.

Remarks: As a noun, *bitchass* is one word; as an adjective, *bitch-ass* is hyphenated.

Example: That *bitchass* just ran away.

Example: That *bitch-ass* dude started crying and ran away.

B

bitchface/bitch face

Part of Speech: noun

Definition: a neutral expression construed as unfriendly or mean in some way, and it's usually preceded by the word *resting*.

Remarks: It can be one word or two. As always, whichever you choose, stick with it.

bitchfit/bitch fit

Part of Speech: noun

Definition: a fit pitched by a person.

Remarks: This term was made famous by the 2004 movie *White Chicks*.

B

bullshit

Part of Speech: noun/verb

Definition: *n.* nonsense, foolishness.

v. when a person who doesn't know what the fuck they're talking about tries to talk around a subject to someone, but that someone is usually intimately familiar with what they're trying to explain.

Remarks: Have you ever heard the phrase, "Can't *bullshit* a bullshitter?"

B

bullshitter

Part of Speech: noun

Definition: a person who doesn't know what the fuck they're talking about, but they try to talk around a subject to someone who is usually intimately familiar with what they're trying to explain.

Remarks: Though you can't bullshit a *bullshitter*, you can certainly go apeshit on the *bullshitter* in question when they're done spewing their shit.

B

butt fucker

Part of Speech: noun

Definition: a vulgar term for someone who performs anal sex.

Remarks: This is pretty vulgar. I wouldn't use this term, but it's in this book because it should be two words, not one, and not hyphenated either.

C

chickenshit

Part of Speech: noun/adjective

Definition: *n.* a person who's being a coward and weak.

adj. chicken, yellow-bellied, cowardly, weak.

Remarks: When this word is used to describe a person, it's one word; it's two words when describing chicken feces.

clusterfuck

Part of Speech: noun

Definition: an overwhelming situation piled on top of more shit, creating an incomprehensible number of ordeals that can't possibly be gone through in a reasonable amount of time; a bad situation involving lots of little circumstances that add up to one huge, crazy-ass problem.

Remarks: That entire process was one big *clusterfuck*!

Clusterfuck is always one word. Don't let anyone tell you any different.

C

cock

Part of Speech: noun

Definition: penis, dick. You know what it is. It's also a male adult chicken.

Remarks: *Cock* rhymes with *rock*. Coincidence?

C

cockblock

Part of Speech: verb

Definition: when someone prevents another person from having sex; sometimes used figuratively, it can also be when someone blocks another person from achieving something they desire, even if it's not sexual in nature, such as a promotion.

Remarks: It's all one word, as are all variations, such as *cockblocked*, *cockblocking*, and *cockblocker*.

C

cockgoblin/cock goblin

Part of Speech: noun

Definition: someone who sucks cock and enjoys it.

Remarks: I've never actually heard someone say this word out loud before. How strange.

C

cocksucker

Part of Speech: noun

Definition: someone who sucks cock; rude insult like *asshole.*

Remarks: That *cocksucker* hung up on me!

C

cold-ass

Part of Speech: adjective

Definition: cold-hearted; very cold, freezing.

Remarks: I've heard this said both ways–*cold-ass* bitch and a *cold-ass* room or *cold-ass* feet. I've heard my husband use the latter on many occasions. It's true–my feet are always cold.

C

crap

Part of Speech: noun

Definition: poop, shit, excrement; another word for *stuff*; an exclamation when something goes wrong.

Remarks: *Crap* is a nicer way of saying *shit*, so if a character in a manuscript says *shit* and it sounds peculiar, try *crap* on for size.

C

crappy

Part of Speech: adjective

Definition: terrible, awful, the worst.

Remarks: You're having a *crappy* day when you get a flat tire on your way to the hospital with your sick husband and sick child. True story.

C

craptastic

Part of Speech: adjective

Definition: the crappiest of the crappy, hardly believable it's so crappy.

Remarks: Regarding the remark for the previous entry, that day was, in fact, a *craptastic* clusterfuck.

C

crazy ass/crazy-ass

Part of Speech: noun/adjective

Definition: *n.* a person who acts a bit on the crazy side.

adj. crazy or extreme.

Remarks: When you're talking about a person, it's two words but should never refer to someone's mental health. It's hyphenated when used as a compound adjective, such as a *crazy-ass* movie.

C

cuckold/cuck

Part of Speech: noun/verb

Definition: *n.* a person who receives sexual gratification from watching their partner have sex with others; a weak person, often used contemptuously to refer to an individual with progressive and liberal views; a person who fears the loss of what is important to them, namely in a political sense.

v. watching a sexual partner have sex with another person; taking away from, as in a country that has been metaphorically taken away from a specific political party.

Continued on next page.

cuckold/cuck (continued from previous page)

Remarks:

The original definition of the word *cuckold* is the first one stated in this entry, but it's taken on new meaning in political arenas in the past decade, hence the other definitions listed on the previous page.

The word *cuck* is the shortened form of *cuckold*. As a verb, each can be modified as follows: *cuckolded* and *cucked* (past tense) or *cuckolding* and *cucking* (present participle).

I do not endorse any political affiliations or beliefs. The choice to include these types of words is simply for educational purposes.

C

cunt

Part of Speech: noun

Definition: a word used to describe a person when the word *bitch* just doesn't cut it because the person is so utterly contemptible; also refers to female genitalia.

Remarks: I rarely use this word, but it's a great sentence enhancer in fiction to convey strong character emotion.

D

dafuq

Part of Speech: interjection

Definition: another way to say, "What the fuck?"

Remarks: Sometimes people shorten this exclamation to "the fuck?" or "da fuck?" and other times it's shortened further, which is why *dafuq* was added to this dicktionary.

D

dammit

Part of Speech: interjection

Definition: an exclamation; a variation of *damn it*, which is also correct, but *dammit* is recommended most of the time unless a person is enunciating each word to make a solid point (great for character dialogue).

Remarks: I thought about adding *dammit all* and *dammit all to hell* to this list, but it just seemed a bit redundant, so they're in this sentence for your reference, spelled correctly and everything. You're welcome.

D

damn

Part of Speech: noun/verb/adjective/adverb

Definition: *n.* a miniscule measure of care and/or consideration for a thing or a person, as in "don't give a *damn.*"

v. to condemn, curse, or ridicule publicly.

adj. absolute or complete, as in "*damn* fool."

adv. there's really no other way to define *damn* as an adverb other than to use its most notorious synonym, *very*.

Remarks: As Mark Twain once said, "Substitute '*damn*' every time you're inclined to write 'very'; your editor will delete it and the writing will be just as it should be." It's true–we're not big fans of the word *very*.

dick

Part of Speech: noun/verb

Definition: *n.* this is obviously a penis, but it can also refer to someone who is abrasive or mean.

v. to take advantage of; to mistreat or to goof off and waste time, as in "Quit *dicking* around!"

Remarks: As a verb, it can be *dick* (present tense), *dicked* (past tense), or *dicking* (present participle).

D

dickbag

Part of Speech: noun

Definition: a combination of *dickhead* and *douchebag*; an annoying or rude individual; a total jerk who is offensive and abrasive and thinks highly of themself when hardly anyone else does.

Remarks: Since *dickhead* and *douchebag* are each displayed as one word–not two, and not hyphenated–the same goes for *dickbag*.

D

dickhead

Part of Speech: noun

Definition: an annoying or rude individual.

Remarks: You may be tempted to write this out as two words, but you'd be wrong. For clarity's sake, it's one word.

D

dipshit

Part of Speech: noun

Definition: a completely incompetent person.

Remarks: I almost forgot to add this word to the list because I rarely use it. I guess I don't know many *dipshits*.

D

douchebag

Part of Speech: noun

Definition: a total jerk who is offensive and abrasive and thinks highly of themself when hardly anyone else does; a bag used for douches.

Remarks: I'm noticing a trend here. There are a lot of words that mean pretty much the same thing—*asshole*, *dick*, and so on.

D

douche canoe

Part of Speech: noun

Definition: a person who goes well beyond being a douchebag.

Remarks: I had heard this expletive once or twice, but a friend wanted me to add it to this list. You're welcome, friend.

D

dumbass

Part of Speech: noun/adjective

Definition: *n.* an idiot; a foolish person.

adj. senseless, thoughtless.

Remarks: "That *dumbass* changed lanes without signaling." My friend Shari came up with this example sentence.

dumbfuck

Part of Speech: noun

Definition: a person who is extraordinarily nonsensical and imprudent.

Remarks: I'm guilty of using this word frequently. I won't say in what context or about whom, but just know it's well deserved.

F

fan-fucking-tastic

Part of Speech: adjective

Definition: a more profane yet enthusiastic way of saying fantastic or great; an ironic way of saying things aren't going so well.

Remarks: Hyphens are needed because, oftentimes, without them it takes a minute for readers to know what word they're reading, and you don't want your audience getting tripped up while reading your story.

Think of it this way: Which of the following would you rather read?

"Damn, that movie was fanfuckingtastic!"

or

"Damn, that movie was *fan-fucking-tastic*!"

F

fuck

Part of Speech: noun/verb/interjection

Definition: *n.* a miniscule measure of care and/or consideration for a thing or a person, as in "don't give a *fuck*."

v. to have sex; to make a mess of things; to screw someone over.

interj. an expression of dismay, resentment, or dissatisfaction.

Remarks: This word can be used in lots of different ways—on its own, as a prefix, as a suffix, and sometimes in the middle of a word, as you saw in the previous entry *and* the very first entry.

F

fuck all

Part of Speech: noun

Definition: nothing.

Remarks: I've seen this written as one word because it sounds like it could be, but it's not. Don't do it!

F

fuckboy

Part of Speech: noun

Definition: a fragile yet selfish person who will say or do anything to have sex while simultaneously doing the bare minimum to achieve that goal; however, it depends on who's saying this word and their intent.

Remarks: The term *fuckboy* was first introduced by a rapper named Cam'ron, and it simply referred to a dude who sucks. From there the term became popular and began taking on new meaning.

F

fuck buddy/fuck-buddy

Part of Speech: noun

Definition: a sexual partner without the emotional attachment; a booty call.

Remarks: Don't mistake a *fuck buddy* for a friend with benefits. *Fuck buddies* aren't always friends too.

F

fuckedupness/fuckedupedness

Part of Speech: noun

Definition: the state or condition of being fucked up.

Remarks: I've heard this one a multitude of times in my life, and sometimes from my own mouth. Note that there are no hyphens in either word. It just looks silly with hyphens, and it's more work. Nobody wants that.

F

fuckening

Part of Speech: noun

Definition: when the day is going well, and then something terrible happens that ruins it.

Remarks: This word is typically preceded by the word *the*. *The fuckening* has been floating around social media for a while now, so I thought I'd give it the attention it deserves by adding it to this dicktionary.

fucker

Part of Speech: noun

Definition: general insult; a little shit or an idiot.

Remarks: Though many sources also define *fucker* as the person who is doing the fucking, the word is rarely used in this manner unless preceded by another word.

F

fuckery

Part of Speech: noun

Definition: a person, place, or thing that is either ridiculous and nonsensical or insidious and deceitful.

Remarks: *Tomfoolery* and *bullshit* are great synonyms for *fuckery*, as in "What tomfoolery is this?" You can also say, "What *fuckery* is this?" or "What bullshit is this?" There is a lot of versality with cursing.

F

fuckface

Part of Speech: noun

Definition: an annoying person; a person whose mere presence irritates you to your core, sometimes for no reason at all.

Remarks: I've known a few *fuckfaces* in my lifetime. I'm a good judge of character, so if I meet someone and automatically think *fuckface*, they probably are.

F

fucking A/fuckin' A

Part of Speech: idiom

Definition: something a person says to affirm what someone else has said; agreeing with someone.

Remarks: Another way to say this without being as derogatory is "Hell yeah!"

F

fucking/fuckin'/fucken/friggin'

Part of Speech: verb/adjective/adverb

Definition: *v.* having sexual relations, intercourse.

adj. an intensifier that describes a noun in a profane manner, such as "that *fucking* asshole."

adv. an intensifier that describes an adjective in a profane manner, such as "That's just *fucking* great!"

Remarks: The other variations of the word listed above can be used in place of *fucking*:
"That *fuckin'* asshole!"
"That *fucken* asshole!"
"That *friggin'* asshole!"
"That's just *fuckin'* great!"
"That's just *fucken* great!"
"That's just *friggin'* great!"

If used in dialogue, think about the way a character speaks, and read the line out loud. Does the character enunciate their words, or is their tone and demeanor more causal? Writers, knowing your characters makes all the difference.

fuck me/fuck-me

Part of Speech: interjection/adjective

Definition: *interj*. an exclamation of frustration or exasperation and sometimes surprise or dismay.

adj. alluring, seductive, enticing, typically when it comes to clothing, especially shoes (pumps/heels).

Remarks: Hyphenated, *fuck-me* is a compound adjective when it precedes a noun. (E.g., "These are my *fuck-me* heels.")

fuck my life (FML)

Part of Speech: idiom

Definition: something a person says when things don't go their way or when someone is having a bad day.

Remarks: *Fuck my life*! My mother is going to *hate* this book.

fucknut/fuck nut

Part of Speech: noun

Definition: something one calls a person who is so foolish and utterly absurd that calling them such isn't good enough.

Remarks: Though this can be spelled as one word or two, my recommendation is to spell it as one word—for no reason other than it is more aesthetically pleasing.

F

fuck off

Part of Speech: idiom

Definition: dismissing someone impolitely; telling a person to go away in a vulgar manner.

Remarks: When I say this, it's usually in a teasing manner.

F

fuck's sake

Part of Speech: idiom

Definition: a reaction to an unpleasant situation when your patience is wearing thin because things haven't been going your way and is typically preceded by the word *for*.

Remarks: Oh, for *fuck's sake*! Not another word with *fuck* in it.

Don't lose your patience just yet. Note that the apostrophe in *fuck's sake* is necessary because *fuck* in this instance is a noun; therefore, the word *fuck* is a possessive noun that takes an apostrophe.

F

fucktard

Part of Speech: noun

Definition: a moron of the highest level.

Remarks: I had reservations about including this word because of how it came to be, but it's in this dicktionary because I've seen it as two words before, and that's incorrect. Please avoid using this word, though. If you have sensitivity readers, they'll tell you the same.

F

fuck-ton

Part of Speech: noun

Definition: in terms of measurement or quantity, a lot.

Remarks: My daughter is gonna have a *fuck-ton* of homework once she gets to high school. Sadly, since I'm The Werd Nerd and not a math geek, I'll be of no use to her when it comes to expressions and equations.

F

fuckup/fuck up/fuck-up

Part of Speech: noun/verb

Definition: *n*. someone who is incompetent and makes lots of mistakes; a blunder or a mistake, sometimes an embarrassing one.

v. to ruin something with carelessness or incompetency.

Remarks: Use *fuckup* or *fuck-up* when you're talking about a person. Use whichever spelling you choose consistently throughout your work, such as a manuscript or an article. When you're saying a situation is *fucked up* or that somebody is going to *fuck up*, it's styled as two words.

F

fuck you

Part of Speech: idiom

Definition: I'm sure we all know this one, but this is a dicktionary, so when someone says this to you, they're pretty much telling you to go to hell.

Remarks: Just like *fuck off*, I typically say this one jokingly too.

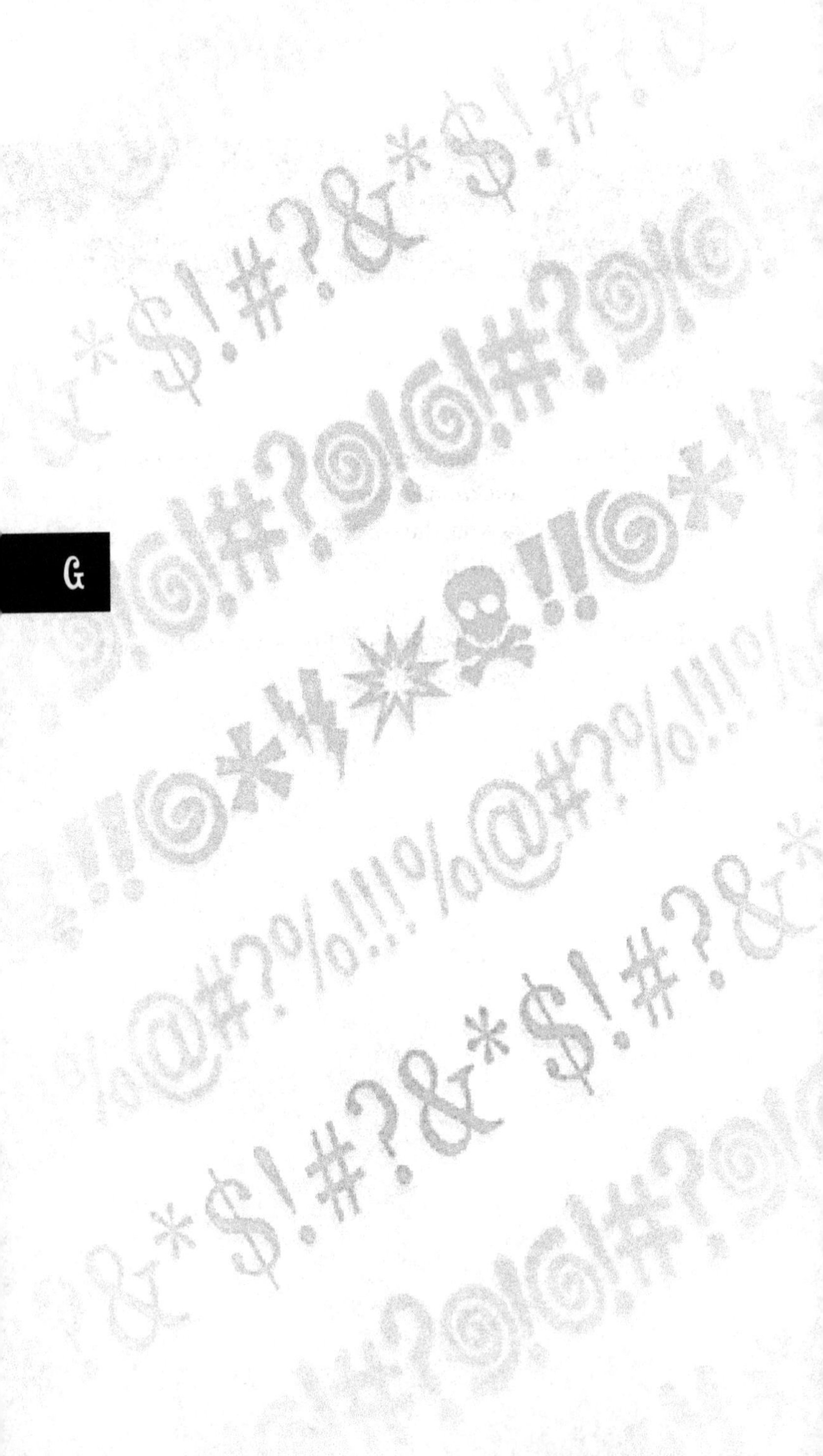

goddammit

Part of Speech: interjection

Definition: an exclamation to express anger, annoyance, or any other similarly heightened emotion.

Remarks: Since I was raised in a home with a Christian mother and a foulmouthed dad who was running from God, I have mixed emotions about this curse word—and a plethora of other things I won't get into. It's in this book because it's one word and it does *not* have an *n* in it, unlike the next word.

G

goddamn/God damn

Part of Speech: interjection/noun/verb

Definition: *interj.* an exclamation of frustration or exasperation.

n. a miniscule measure of care and/or consideration for a thing or a person, as in "don't give a *goddamn*."

v. to condemn, curse, or ridicule.

Remarks: This should be one word when a character in a book you're writing/editing is frustrated to the point of not caring how their words come out. When a character is enunciating each word they say to get their point across, it's advised to use the two-word variation.

For instance, "*God damn* you, Sylvester." She spoke the words slowly while maintaining unwavering eye contact.

hell-bent

Part of Speech: adjective

Definition: determined in a stubborn and oftentimes reckless manner.

Remarks: I am *hell-bent* on selling thousands upon thousands of copies of this dicktionary.

H

hellhole

Part of Speech: noun

Definition: a place that is shitty beyond belief or recognition, a pigsty; a terrible place to live or to be in general.

Remarks: You may be tempted to write this out as two words, but as one word, the full effect of the definition solidifies its claim.

H

helluva

Part of Speech: adverbial intensifier

Definition: another way to spell "hell of a," as in "That was one hell of a party!"

Remarks: If a character in a book you're writing/editing has had just a tad too much to drink, they may slur their words, so it may come out as "That's one *helluva* party, man!"

horseshit

Part of Speech: noun

Definition: nonsense, balderdash, rubbish, or foolery.

Remarks: My dad's friend used to say, "*Horseshit* and applesauce." I'm not sure he used it in the correct context, but this book is dedicated to my dad, so it's relevant nonetheless.

J

jackass

Part of Speech: noun

Definition: someone who lacks judgment.

Remarks: There's a television series and movie series with this title.

J

jack shit

Part of Speech: noun

Definition: anything, as in "he doesn't know anything"; a lack of knowledge.

Remarks: I don't know *jack shit* about math except that numbers are involved.

K

kickass/kick ass/kick-ass

Part of Speech: noun/verb/adjective

Definition: *n.* someone or something that is awesome and possibly unbeatable.

v. to win at something; to hurt someone.

adj. cool, awesome.

Remarks: As a noun, it's one word; as a verb, it's two words; and as an adjective, it's hyphenated.

"That's *kickass!*" People rarely say this anymore. They tend to say *badass* instead, but *kickass* is one of its synonyms.

"He's gonna *kick ass* today," is a common phrase to say someone will do well.

"Those are some *kick-ass* shoes." This takes us back to *-ass.* It can be added to the ends of many words, and when it is, the entire word typically becomes an adjective, like it is in this sentence.

M

mindfuck

Part of Speech: noun/verb

Definition: *n.* something mind-boggling or jarring.

v. to cause mental manipulation, inflicting confusion or distress of some kind.

Remarks: When I say *mindfuck*, I'm typically referring to movies that mess with the mind, like psychological thrillers, as in "That movie was a total *mindfuck*" or "I've just been *mindfucked*."

motherfucker (mofo)

Part of Speech: noun

Definition: a term for a person that can be used in a derogatory manner, as a compliment, or comparatively.

Remarks: This is one of the most versatile curses around because it can be said about pretty much anyone.

As an insult: "That *motherfucker* stole my chips."

As a compliment: "That's one badass *motherfucker*."

Comparative: "That dude is high as a *motherfucker*."

P

piss off/pissed off/pissed-off

Part of Speech: verb/adjective

Definition: *v*. to anger or infuriate.

adj. with a hyphen, this is a compound adjective that describes displaying anger.

Remarks: Though this isn't necessarily a cuss word/phrase, I've seen *pissoff*, and that's incorrect.

Pissed-off is a compound adjective that is followed by the noun it modifies, as in a "*pissed-off* cheerleader." Don't hyphenate it when it comes after the noun, such as "the cheerleader was *pissed off*."

P

piss-poor

Part of Speech: adjective

Definition: broke, impoverished; poor quality; terrible.

Remarks: Words to live by: Don't be a *piss-poor* excuse for a human being.

P

pussy

Part of Speech: noun

Definition: vagina; a wimp.

Remarks: I'm not particularly a fan of this word, and I'm not sure why exactly. I mean, I have no problem with the word *cunt*. Strange.

P

pussy-whipped

Part of Speech: adjective

Definition: bending to the will of a significant other because sex is being used as a bargaining chip.

Remarks: The word *whipped* alone can also be used to say the same thing.

quief

Part of Speech: noun

Definition: a vaginal fart that occurs from built-up pressure, namely after sex.

Remarks: This isn't necessarily an expletive, but since it's commonly misspelled and vulgar, I thought I'd add it for shits and giggles.

shart

Part of Speech: noun/verb

Definition: *n.* a fart that is so powerful a person shits themselves.

v. farting so hard, one shits themself.

Remarks: This word is a combination of the word *shit* and the word *fart*. Clever. If you've never *sharted*, you've clearly never been shit-faced.

S

shit

Part of Speech: noun/verb/interjection

Definition: *n.* poop, feces, dung; the act of pooping; crap or nonsense; teasing remarks; poor or unfair conduct; random stuff.

v. to poop; to deceive or *try* to deceive someone.

interj. an exclamation of frustration or exasperation and sometimes surprise or dismay.

Remarks: As a noun, *shit* can pretty much be anything. It's one of the most versatile words in this dicktionary.

For instance, "While I was *shitting*, my roommate was yelling some *shit* from the other room about how I *always* leave my work *shit* on the table."

S

shitbag

Part of Speech: noun

Definition: scumbag; an indecent, putrid human being.

Remarks: I would never call my husband a *shitbag*. He's the most decent man I know.

shitballs

Part of Speech: interjection

Definition: an exclamation of excitement or frustration, or of anything really.

Remarks: I don't know if it's common for most folks to use this word, but I do, so it's relevant.

shitcan/shit-can

Part of Speech: verb

Definition: to fire someone from their current position of employment.

Remarks: The past tense is spelled one of two ways: *shitcanned* or *shit-canned.* Just remember, you can't use both spellings in a manuscript or in a series of books. You must choose only one. If you want my two cents, go with *shitcan/shitcanned.*

shit-eating

Part of Speech: adjective

Definition: smug, boastful, egotistic, and typically followed by the noun *grin*.

Remarks: I'll be wearing a *shit-eating* grin once this dicktionary hits the shelves.

shit-faced

Part of Speech: noun

Definition: drunk out of one's mind.

Remarks: Though I don't get *shit-faced* anymore, I don't have a problem watching others get *shit-faced*. In fact, it's pretty entertaining.

shitfit/shit fit/shit-fit

Part of Speech: noun

Definition: a tantrum, freak-out.

Remarks: There are three ways this can be spelled—as one word, two, or hyphenated. As I've said many times throughout this book already, you can't have them all. Choose one way of spelling it and stay consistent.

S

shitfuck

Part of Speech: interjection

Definition: an exclamation of frustration or exasperation and sometimes surprise or dismay.

Remarks: This word likely originated with someone who didn't know if they should yell *shit* or *fuck*, so they decided both were necessary. I've had those days.

S

shithead

Part of Speech: noun

Definition: someone who has either just done something really stupid or is always a complete imbecile.

Remarks: I can't even tell you how many times I've called a former boss a *shithead*—not to their face, of course. Now when I think my boss is a *shithead*, I can actually do something about it. I love being my own boss!

shithole

Part of Speech: noun

Definition: a place that is shitty and filthy beyond belief or recognition, a pigsty; a terrible place to live or to be in general.

Remarks: You may be tempted to write this out as two words, but as one word, the full effect of the definition solidifies its claim.

shitload

Part of Speech: noun

Definition: far too much of something.

Remarks: As an editor, I've accumulated a *shitload* of reading material over the years.

shitshow/shit show/shit-show

Part of Speech: noun

Definition: a metaphoric trainwreck; a completely awful and messy situation.

Remarks: I'm sure we can all agree that the year 2020 was a complete *shitshow*! Unless you want your work to be a complete *shitshow* too, use only one form of this word throughout your text.

S

shit stain

Part of Speech: noun

Definition: a streak or smear of feces on the inside of underwear; an abhorrent individual who can be likened to that of shit on underwear.

Remarks: I've never been so disgusted with someone that I've called them a *shit stain.*

S

shitstorm

Part of Speech: noun

Definition: a tumultuous sequence of events that spirals out of control; a difficult and/or chaotic situation.

Remarks: This is a compound word that is rarely written as two words, which is why there is only one variation listed here.

shit talk

Part of Speech: noun/verb

Definition: *n.* criticism; smack talk.

v. talking trash about someone, either to their face or behind their back.

Remarks: Whether you use this term in the present tense, past tense, or as a present participle, it's displayed as two words–not one word and not hyphenated: *shit talks*, *shit talked*, and *shit talking*.

Please note that if you leave the *g* off the present participle, you'll need to add an apostrophe after the *n*–*shit talkin'*. The same goes for any verb ending in *ing*.

S

shitter

Part of Speech: noun

Definition: toilet, commode.

Remarks: Sage advice: No one should disturb a man while he's on the *shitter*. It's his personal time.

S

shit-ton

Part of Speech: noun

Definition: in terms of measurement or quantity, a lot.

Remarks: Luckily, I don't have a *shit-ton* of work to do today, so I'm working on this dicktionary.

slut

Part of Speech: noun

Definition: a person who has sex with multiple people, and there's usually no emotional involvement.

Remarks: I used to call one of my exes a *slut*. It was true at the time, so he would just shrug. But, don't call anyone a *slut*; it's fucking rude.

S

smartass/smart-ass

Part of Speech: noun/adjective

Definition: *n.* a pretentious wise guy who typically states the obvious in a sarcastically demeaning or condescending manner.

adj. describes the act of stating the obvious or not-so-obvious in an exaggerated and sarcastic manner, and typically precedes a noun, such as *remark*.

Remarks: As a noun, write it out as one word—*smartass*—and hyphenate it when it's an adjective—*smart-ass*. By the way, I highly encourage *smart-ass* reviews of this book.

S

son of a bitch

Part of Speech: phrasal noun/interjection

Definition: *n.* a term used to describe a person who is mean or even haughty; a term used to refer to any number of things, as in "the controller just died on him, so he threw the *son of a bitch* across the room."

interj. an exclamation of frustration or exasperation and sometimes surprise or dismay.

Remarks: The plural form is *sons of bitches*, but a lot of times when people say it, they don't enunciate each and every syllable. With that said, if a character in a book you're writing or editing says or thinks this, it'll likely be spelled *sonsabitches*. I know I've said it before, but writers, knowing your characters makes all the difference.

S

sweet-ass

Part of Speech: adjective

Definition: describing something that is awesome, typically when it precedes a noun.

Remarks: Maybe I'll get myself a *sweet-ass* ride after I sell a million copies of this book. Hey, a girl can dream, right?

Of course, there's also *sweet ass*, as in "she has a *sweet ass*," but that would technically get filed under the entry for *ass/-ass*.

thundercunt

Part of Speech: noun

Definition: a cunt, but worse—a major fucking cunt.

Remarks: If the word *cunt* doesn't even come close to what you want to call a bitch, try *thundercunt* on for size. It's like slapping someone twice—no, thrice!

As I type this out, I'm thinking of the song by AC/DC that begins with the word *thunder*, and I'm substituting some of the lyrics in the original song. It really sets the tone for writing this book. Too bad we're nearing the end.

twat

Part of Speech: noun

Definition: vagina; a person who's irksome and frustrating to a degree of annoyance.

Remarks: I rarely hear *twat* in reference to a female body part, and I advise against it.

T

twatwaffle

Part of Speech: noun

Definition: a person who's irksome and frustrating to a degree of annoyance.

Remarks: Yes, *twat* and *twatwaffle* have the same definition. The only difference between the two is some syrupy goodness.

un-fucking-believable

Part of Speech: adverb

Definition: a variant of the word *unbelievable*, which means that something is truly hard to believe because it seems unconvincing or implausible.

Remarks: Like the first word in this dicktionary (*abso-fucking-lutely*), *un-fucking-believable* is a hyphenated compound word. Reader satisfaction decreases when hyphens aren't used in this manner because *unfuckingbelievable* is an eyesore without those hyphens!

whore

Part of Speech: noun

Definition: a person who has sex for money.

Remarks: Though this can also be a verb, I did not add that definition here, namely because this term is offensive to those who have sex for money. The appropriate term is *sex worker* and should be used instead.

ACKNOWLEDGMENTS

There are a few people who helped make this book possible, and what follows is my thanks to each of them.

I am grateful to my husband for his patience while I wrote this book. Every time I heard a cuss word in a television show or a movie, I would say, "Oh, is that on the list?" The man has the patience of a saint, and not for this reason alone.

My daughter is a great motivator. Throughout my editing career, she's told me that I will one day write a book, and though it's not fiction–and she won't be able to read this book for a few years–she was right. I'm sure I'll hear "I told you so" for years to come.

Alex Galassi–one of my clients–inspired this book with a character in his sci-fi/fantasy novel, *Battle for Eklatros*. Said character is a privateer who cusses like a sailor–pun intended–but he's got a good heart.

Another client continued to inspire the list of vulgarities with his action/adventure novel. As I was editing the second book in Ron Lamberson's *Kilimanjaro Club Adventure* series, I came across more swear words, and they, too, were added to this book.

Thank you to Carly for her honest feedback and her awkward queries. Choosing Carly as my editor was the best decision I made throughout this entire process. We sure had a blast going back and forth with this dicktionary.

Thanks to Polly Letofsky of My Word Publishing for her time and wisdom. Without her coaching me through copyright law and other very specific details in the publishing process, such as the ins and outs of KDP, I'd be lost.

The interior design and layout would be drab and boring if not for the brilliance of talented interior layout designer Victoria Wolf of Wolf Design & Marketing. Her vision breathed life into this dicktionary, inside and out.

Thanks to all of my friends for holding their tongues before the book release and for putting up with my shenanigans while this book was being written. We certainly had some giggles.

Last, but certainly not least, thank you for your support, dear reader. I made this book for you, and I hope it aids you for many years to come.

ABOUT THE AUTHOR

Erika M. Weinert is a copy and line editor who lives in the Pacific Northwest (PNW) and is an active member of the Northwest Editors Guild—a regional, industry-specific association of editors. She mentors fledgling editors through the guild and on her own. When she's not providing remote editing services to her clients and mentoring, Erika can be found at home with her family. She has a wonderful husband who is thoughtful, sensitive, and a great father to their daughter, whom they brought into the world the same year they were married—2008. Their daughter is a typical teen, but she's also selfless, empathetic, and more self-aware than her mother was at that age. Erika treasures her family—including their two cats—and her career above all else.

CPSIA information can be obtained
at www.ICGtesting.com
Printed in the USA
LVHW081649280922
729506LV00008B/778